ALIEN MATTER

Regina Derieva

SELECTED POEMS BY REGINA DERIEVA, TRANSLATED BY VARIOUS HANDS
(ALAN SHAW, RICHARD MCKANE, KEVIN CAREY, PETER FRANCE,
ANDREY GRITSMAN, ILYA BERNSTEIN, AND ROBERT REID)

Edited by Hildred Crill

SPUYTEN DUYVIL
NEW YORK CITY

copyright © 2005 Regina Derieva
Respective translations copyrighted © 2005
cover painting: *Creation* by Arcady Kotler
ISBN 1-933132-22-1

Library of Congress Cataloging-in-Publication Data

Derieva, Regina.
[Sobranie dorog. English]
Alien matter : new and selected poems / Regina Derieva ; translated by various hands, Alan Shaw ... [et al.] ; edited by Hildred Crill.
p. cm.
ISBN-13: 978-1-933132-22-8
ISBN-10: 1-933132-22-1
1. Derieva, Regina--Translations into English. I. Shaw, Alan.
II. Crill, Hildred. III. Title.
PG3479.6.E73S6613 2005
891.71'44--dc22
2005020341

Contents

Absence: Poems 1978-1994

At the Intersection / tr. Richard McKane
Sum of Associations / tr. Peter France
Eyes Sticky With Sleep, It's So Early / tr. Richard McKane
No Need to Explain to Me / tr. Richard McKane
Conversation With Myself, Year 1985 / tr. Richard McKane
Spring and Autumn / tr. Kevin Carey
The House is Rickety as an Old Man's Tooth / tr. Richard McKane
Monuments are Lies / tr. Andrey Gritsman
I Don't Feel at Home Where I Am / tr. Alan Shaw
Maxims and Paradoxes on the Accidental Sheets / tr. Kevin Carey
The Age Was Iron: It's Gone to Rust / tr. Alan Shaw
Tormenting Songs for One Traveling in Latvia / tr. Richard McKane
Prior to Departure / tr. Ilya Bernstein
Shut a Final Door / tr. Kevin Carey
Everything You Need to Know / tr. Kevin Carey
Only to Walk to the Sea of Pines / tr. Richard McKane
Qui Pro Quo / tr. Andrey Gritsman
The Land of Ur / tr. Robert Reid
The Art of Photography / tr. Richard McKane

The Last War: Poems 1995-1998

Inverse Perspective / tr. Peter France
What Kind of Thing is Time — An Attic, a Barracks, a Jail / tr. Ilya Bernstein
Russian Album / tr. Andrey Gritsman
The Venous Snow, Swollen Snowdrifts / tr. Andrey Gritsman
Autumn Tirade / tr. Andrey Gritsman
Winter Tirade / tr. Robert Reid
No Dream Can Wake You Up, But Wake You Must / tr. Ilya Bernstein
For G.G. / tr. Richard McKane
A Fragment of Culture II / tr. Richard McKane
Winter Lectures for Terrorists / tr. Kevin Carey

Fugitive Space: Poems 1999-2001

The Cast-off Remnant of a Centaur / tr. Alan Shaw
For P. O. / tr. Richard McKane
Winter. Euterpe / tr. Alan Shaw
It Was Not Necessary to Study / tr. Kevin Carey
But if There is a Bomb? / tr. Kevin Carey
And No One Can Tell About It / tr. Kevin Carey
Since I Have Not Had My Home / tr. Kevin Carey

Of All Things to Do / tr. Kevin Carey
That's About it or The Theory of Relativity / tr. Kevin Carey
Detail / tr. Kevin Carey
Another Side of the Matter / tr. Kevin Carey
In the Beginning. At the End / tr. Kevin Carey
Pricked by the Pin / tr. Kevin Carey
The Diagnosis / tr. Kevin Carey
I Have Rolled Myself Up / tr. Kevin Carey
The Anatomical Poetry Theatre / tr. Richard McKane
Imitation of the Ancient / tr. Richard McKane
Commemoration of Alexander Blok / tr. Richard McKane
For I. Yefimov / tr. Andrey Gritsman

Recent Poems 2002-2003

Spring Harangue / tr. Ilya Bernstein
Whether I turn to the shooting star or the tear / tr. Ilya Bernstein
We Will All Turn Into Salt, as God Wished / tr. Richard McKane
In the Absence of Causes / tr. Ilya Bernstein
To Whom it May Concern / tr. Alan Shaw
East Norwalk, CT / tr. Alan Shaw
Direction / tr. Ilya Bernstein
What is an Apple? The Eye of the Apple / tr. Ilya Bernstein
The Last Island / tr. Ilya Bernstein

Absence: Poems 1978-1994

AT THE INTERSECTION

It's not possible to exaggerate...
  E. Montale

1.

I would walk in step with time
but I limp a little. As a result
I carry out my monologue from a corner,
(from a hole if you like). By the way,

there is a prospect of the desert. I put
my arms behind my back, shorten my step.
I arouse instinct in the old lags,
that is the beasts whose times are without term.

I should remember I am a human being
but the wild wind prevents me
and the happy children of the guards
look out from under marble eyelids.

2.

I went in and looked at the walls,
no change had touched them.
The conclusion is there's no
plus marks there.
How to tears the sting out of rumor,
how not to scratch midge bites?
The hook hung below the ceiling
was the question mark of the playwright
(was he or was he not)? Without
the services of a desperately unpaid surgeon
it wouldn't have worked out.

"And where's the anaesthetic?"
It wasn't considered necessary to inject
the vein, I didn't get to be in the kingdom
of dreams, the soul didn't ask permission
for change. Pain overcomes the axiom
that humans are zeros —
they're less, and homesickness
no longer torments them.
Walls remind them
of prison, of hospital — that subject
that thinks with the formula of betrayal.

3.

I lived on the flat surface
and I lost the keys of the city in my haste.
Now I cannot go there, of course.
Can any thing be allowed a pawn?

It stands on the black and white board
until it's taken off by the chance move of things.
From there arises a longing for wood,
international as autumn.

What can a pawn do? Absolutely nothing.
Although there is a chance of rolling off somewhere,
of cramming into a crack and celebrating Christmas
with some rusted knitting-needle.

On slow, wooden roots
I shall return to my square in a square.
In the end game, which proceeds in the dark,
to plunge in thorns for all my brothers,

all my sisters! Who was I?
A wooden rose of the winds and south,
on the flat board, then table,
then earth… an imperceptible threat.

SUM OF ASSOCIATIONS

Life was measured by horizons
in distant eras too.
Measure of grief, measure of exile,
letters from Pontus or the front.

Like a scroll roll out that steppe,
Weep above it, grasshopper.
The steed may raise his hoof,
the rider's shoulders be of lead.

Nearer ocean does not mean nearer
the boat, the deck, the mast. . .
Nothing's immobile, and time threads
the little dachas in the village.

Weeping is drawn out, the space between
is drawn out — so long is time.
Give purple, to wrap the beggar!
Give him a friend, give him a son.

They will give nothing, only weeping.
They will say: no more's allowed.
Door will open: a message for you—
black bread and Black Sea salt.

EYES STICKY WITH SLEEP, IT'S SO EARLY

Eyes sticky with sleep, it's so early.
You go out — it's pitch dark around.
You run, your steps abandoned
as through thickets of tall weeds.

No pretending, no lying.
The wind wheezes like a hanged man,
and every third fence plank
is caught on the run.

You can't weld the hole of the mouth.
The snowstorm having broken its chain
sews space and sows murk,
so that the corner of vision swims.

Let me sleep it off, let me relax
completely, get back my smile.
So that I may get back and disappear,
so I may fall and not rise.

NO NEED TO EXPLAIN TO ME

No need to explain to me
Joseph's bread of captivity.
My existence will wear itself out
in the region of lead-poisoning.

The doorman scrapes the world with his shovel,
he's been killing the snow since early morning.
Life, rich with writing,
is freezing in the yard.

Lips blue from cold,
whisper brothers' names.
You can never get out of a city
where war is forever going on.

CONVERSATION WITH MYSELF, YEAR 1985

God, let me not go out of my mind.
　　　　　　　　　　A. P.

1

And the sea has become the depths, and a part
a particle, but the particle of light
lives and annoys the powers that be
because it lives. It's also of the order
of splinters and specks of dust, the powers
hold down the surgeon and the oculist.
There is so much in the world?
　　　　　　　　　　　"Eh?"
What was Montale on about with his whistle?
How can we communicate in the dark ?
a particle with a part of light, of speech?
Who's there to shout at and to whisper to,
when there's no way of sending a bottle?
Glass is in vain, and sealing wax
too, in vain are the pearls
in the settled feature of heaps and storm clouds.
But something is wandering. A nerve
and particle of light in full darkness,
so Egyptian that it's timely
to howl like a prisoner on death row,
like a dog who doesn't want to run with the pack.

2

The Cretan labyrinth of the mind
can't remember the way out and darkness
persecutes it and horror
is howled out, like a woman without a husband,
like a world without the four points of the compass
that are nailed up crosswise
by hammer and sickle, like a throne
hastily transformed into a dais.

The brain, exiled to the island of Crete,
dressed like a prisoner, shaved
like a convict, does not remember the way out.
It thirsts for damp silence,
blindfolded and the waves lap pianissimo.
What does the brain want
that's gone off the rails into the dark.
The Soviet wind blows outside the windows.
Life has long been boarded up.
Only the boat-hook scrapes the sea's bed
all the way from the island of Crete
and corpses are pulled up in the nets.

3

To pour into the ear the poison of the sentence.
What does the idiot need? Sound sleep:
to fall asleep and dream? There's no reproach
after the injection ... The balcony is open.
"Here, cretin, come here! Here there's not much light,
here the ties of time are really broken!"
What does the idiot need? A blanket,
an injection against fear, and blissful sleep.
Not that, when they opened the closed door,
came in, seized by the throat and murdered,
then did it again. He's not Lazarus, no!
Why rise from the named grave?
Why change the color black to white?
Now the wake, a drinking bout and fancy buns,
at least death was a bit merciful.
Now the idiot will wake and float up from the depths,
now he'll... Returned from the borders of fantasy
he sees the ceiling as his country,
he'll get to know again the flaws and bruises:
a landscape always like the Moon,
where thoughts and lines wandered
                                          with him?

4

The conversation with the idiot took place on Tuesday.
He was looking at the ceiling.
The globe of his head was more neglected
than any crazy idea.
He wandered like heavenly bodies do,
ignoring any question.
Everywhere the nadirs and cosmos
that is to say the grave,
blindness, dumbness.
The veteran of dark rooms, prisoner of failures,
without a hook to hang hope on,
he knew too little for those growing swiftly wiser,
just the intonation and sound.

A useless idiot out of his mind,
a fool beyond all boundaries.
We have to speak loudly — he's hard of hearing:
better whistle or sign.

SPRING AND AUTUMN

Invertebrate freedom,
as wind, for example, or wave...
I'd like such a season,
when a new string tightens,

when pine-tree rasps and weeps
(invents the Russian fleet),
when boarded up are the cottages,
when the jam has sugared,

when winter... Around me
freedom: from center to sick river.
But on my lips only alkaline
solution, and ache of backbone.

THE HOUSE IS RICKETY AS AN OLD MAN'S TOOTH

The house is rickety as an old man's tooth,
its boundaries are bare with wires.
Long ago the creaking hand
has filled the possible blanks.

The pen creaks forming tracks,
fate creaks, searching for a way out,
cripple life creaks, throwing about thoughts
against itself like yellow berries.

They crush this late harvest
and destroy slaughtered Hecuba's house.
And after they say: 'Really, we're sorry,'
with a grin on their snake lips.

MONUMENTS ARE LIES

Monuments are lies
embodied in stone.
And a man — is a lie,
embodied in a body.
When people turn into statues,
they disappear out of sight from other people.
The human counts on love,
but others treat him as a statue, —
they simply don't notice.

I DON'T FEEL AT HOME WHERE I AM

I don't feel at home where I am,
or where I spend time; only where,
beyond counting, there's freedom and calm,
that is, waves, that is, space where, when there,

you consist of pure freedom, which, seen,
turns that Gorgon, the crowd, to stone,
to pebbles and sand . . . where life's mean-
ing lies buried, that never let one

come within cannon shot yet.
From cloud-covered wells untold
pour color and light, a fete
of cupids and Ledas in gold.

That is, silk and honey and sheen.
That is, boon and quiver and call.
That is, all that lives to be free,
needing no words at all.

MAXIMS AND PARADOXES ON THE ACCIDENTAL SHEETS

* * *

All my life
I sought
an angel.
And he appeared
in order to say:
"I am no angel!"

* * *

I live in that year
and in this year.
Time doesn't make
any impression.

* * *

Castles in the air
are built by those
who don't know
what a house is.
They are built
by those who
never had
their own house.

* * *

A poem —
is just one more
scrap of paper
that has sailed off the table
in a bottle
with a cry for help.

* * *

Clouds flying
very quickly.
Oh, how difficult
to read them
in the afternoon
of life.

* * *

If Hamlet
had not made up
Shakespeare,
if Verter
had not made up
Goethe,
if Raskolnikov
had not made up
Dostoevsky,
if J. Alfred Prufrock
had not made up
Eliot,
if Gorbunov and Gorchakov
had not made up
Brodsky,
What would we know
about disenfranchised
persons?

* * *

Space collects
monuments. Time
collects soldiers.
Time protects soldiers
in order to destroy
the monuments.

* * *

Childhood is lost somewhere,
youth is lost somewhere —
happiness,
being carefree...
The memory is lost somewhere,
in order
not to cry.

* * *

I would choose
a word
and fly on it
like on
a balloon.
But it is not permitted
to inflate words.

THE AGE WAS IRON: IT'S GONE TO RUST

The age was iron: it's gone to rust,
corroded over like a knife,
the edge of naked power lost
that had worlds trembling for their life.

A shard of dingy steel remains.
they carefully polish it with sand,
and the awful muscle strains,
with primal impulse, at the hand.

TORMENTING SONGS FOR ONE TRAVELING IN LATVIA

1.

Flat sea with canned fish,
fine sand like dandruff or manna.
A boat without a sail moves
for the distance is inexhaustible and ruddy.

The unforeseen closeness slides along
quickly for the sake of the future, like a cold boat.
The light has not gone dark yet, although they've taken away
the pale blue from which it was sewn.

All trifles of the world are thrown into the sea.
The stubborn twilight of the gods emphasizes
the look that separates from the iris,
like the former borders of the state.

2.

Fish perish, seagulls perish, dunes
also perish. The beach is sprinkled with death.
Fortinbras and his sort of people
collect the corpses by the moonlight.

There is a smell of chlorine, but the smell
of rotting, iodine, fresh collapse is stronger.
One can howl, sitting on one's back paws,
one can enjoy a promenade.

One can do everything, when it's impossible to have a gram,
a soul, a word, a word of advice...
Cosmos, abyss, the pit that's dug
are all overflowing with dead light.

3.

The air puffs up with voices
like a sail: that means the boat will come,
and laughter — a scattered bead,
and day — an amber find,

and all, and the power of the choir will continue,
and life will continue till the next incident...
Layer on layer, pattern on top of pattern,
a butterfly over the barbed wire.

PRIOR TO DEPARTURE

I have a dream that I will not have time
to connect the words, that I will not depart.
Laocoon leans over the serpent and
engages in private conversation.

He persuades and conjures it. He says:
"What do the children have to do with it?"
Since then, the waves have not stopped
beating. Since then, the winds have not stopped blowing.

"What do I have to do with it?" The grip of fate
grows tighter, steeper, closer to the pit.
And the dream torments me, like asthma,
and turns the sky into stone.

SHUT A FINAL DOOR

There's no return to home,
no return for a long time.
There is sealed light,
there is wine with poison.

There is life and death, brother,
beyond the fortress wall.
And Socrates falling down,
on his sick left side.

EVERYTHING YOU NEED TO KNOW

1. *You may think that this is for you*

You still exist.
Somewhere in memory,
you persist
like snow from last winter
which has not yet
thawed.

2. *Teach What You Have to Learn
or Learn What You Have to Forget*

We lived in an iron time:
with an iron trap
they caught iron mice.
In an iron cage
they kept iron birds,
every person they stood
by the nose in the iron corner,
by the knees on the iron peas.
What sort of a bed was there
with the princess's pea !
The bed was made of iron.
On the iron bed lay a mattress
in prisoner's dress;
we had just come out
from the camp or the prison,
had just returned
from the logging area.
Near the iron mattress
there had to be
an iron mug with iron water,

and next to it ?
an iron piece of bread.
Iron Felix looked from the wall
of the iron torture chamber,
unhappy with the paper icon
and the 9-year old child
in the iron boots,
who by his tears was making
the metal corrode.

3. *Because You Know Yourself*

You are always
contemplating diversion
against yourself.
Derailing, for example,
your life.
Exploding, for example,
haunting truth.
Giving away, for example,
the State secret
of your existence.
Destroying, for example,
your roots,
considered as a vestal organ.
Being imprisoned, for example,
because of orders not carried out.
And in general managing to say
just the opposite in everything,
because you consider all the words
as your own property.
You always were by yourself,
how you like to be,
in everybody's absence
and presence.

4. *Do you still believe?*

You are a thought of God
from beyond
all space and time.

5. *I Know You Can Fight*

One lost himself
going down the street
ineffectually throwing up his hands.
"Where am I ?"
It can happen to you.
Summer running through him
like the shaft of an arrow
through St. Sebastian.
If he stopped
bewilderment would tear him.
"Who am I ?"
He staggered along
after his shadow
which became a road-sign
(pointing only to the dark).
"What's the time ?"
It's unimportant
for one who has lost himself.
At present you,
running out of the orbit of life,
will tear into something,
and will explode the connection
between the names.

6. *Your Life is Exactly What Your Thoughts Make It*

You are the coin,
covered with a patina,
which lay in the ground
for over a thousand years.
But nothing can renovate you.
Even sand can't rub you up.
And where is this sand?
In a sun-dial.
And now particles of you
have flowed through my fingers.
Only a flood of consciousness is
still fresh.

ONLY TO WALK TO THE SEA OF PINES

Only to walk to the sea of pines,
only to search for the golden fleece...
You can try to forget prison,
if the eye of the needle is handed to you.

One can try and stitch life and death with paces.
One can look through the needle's eye and sing
something about the ripple and the firmament.

How good it is in the bitter water!
Examine it in profile and full face
through the opening of keen disaster
that has pierced us with exile.

QUI PRO QUO

If one doesn't know the perspective, the hills
cover the distance, but one can climb
Eleon and tear from the beggar's
pouch an even strip of the road's line.

Dirt or snow, it's all the same.
Ecclesiastes had scattered the times
along with stones and previous testament
had not realized what guilt is.

Sea of hills, sea of blood and sea
of the crooked roads, oceans of stones.
If one escapes both alive and dead
one has to live without all roots.

You have to end with the promise of life's
gauge and straighten the tongue,
to end with the fierce and endless fights
and to thrive to the heights where God reigns.

THE LAND OF UR

The land that was is known as Ur,
and something in the land that was
lies hidden from us in a blur,
unknown, beyond our grasp.

Yet something must have been there once,
if only space or passing years;
one can't conceive, unless by sense,
the place where God appears.

Weep, run or be still: I cannot
remember or forget who I
was; I cannot know or unknow
who I am yet to be.

The shepherd tends his sheep again,
the weary distaff guides the yarn,
but from such agonizing shame
no-one on earth can run.

It's forbidden. There was a land.
There is no land. One destiny—
now another. And God demands
a sacrificial country.

THE ART OF PHOTOGRAPHY

                              It's
from a chrysalis, a cocoon, lace,
from wood shavings, not completely aroused,
all stupefied and it looks at itself from the outside.

All frozen, it looks at itself ahead,
to where the aim can spread wings.
Alongside a muslin net lies abandoned—
an object to catch trembles and shudders.

No amateurs thought up yet,
hope for the dawn doesn't fight
with darkness under its cone that drops pollen.
But where flight is there is some madman…

Think about anything but not that, not
about dictatorship or arbitrary rule.
Not about passion which is doubly
senseless on a yellow background of pain.

The Last War: Poems 1995-1998

INVERSE PERSPECTIVE

Air with a pine-tree needle stitches the cavity,
with the same needle mends the seditious sail.
To sail away you must swear loyalty to the sky:
you must fly up to leave behind no traces in the soil.

To sing you must have salt, iodine, the sea;
on the ship's pine-tree you must fly a sail of Greece.
In the hospital corridor you must sew up with metal
your wretched childhood, your old age of poverty.

Between Scylla and Charybdis with a pine-tree's hope
rip open the seam, breathe in at last, and weep.
Not because you remain without sea, without shelter,
but for the dead man gone from the tropic of Dark.

WHAT KIND OF THING IS TIME

What kind of thing is time — an attic, a barracks, a jail,
a borderline, a dirty trick, an evil, a newspaper, a sovereign?...
For him who has shoveled out the burning coals of life,
Time is a boot, a dime.

But the wing of a butterfly is like the hand of a child.
And the turtledove is as cool as a wave.
And fire repeats the stars on earth.
And we can see the ladder from Jacob's dream.

How frightening is time: it pushes the Light away.
How it insists on playing and is tangled up in play.
It has no secrets — that is the only secret
of any span of time, digging a tunnel like a mole.

It is so alien to me, so far from having any use,
that I must climb out of here not backward
and not forward, but upward. Upward, on lines of verse.
On a letter tossed up into the blue, tossed up into the City.

RUSSIAN ALBUM

The palace on the square — Palazzo
(which is the same), thick
cabbage-soup of bushes, clown's laugh
and tears of Russia, motherland.

And common man of the suburbs,
man who is poor and humble.
And life from this news to another
and the battle at unknown Kalka

A short period, infrequent sigh,
fierce vengeful cold, summer quickly passing.
And the shepherd is kind and yet unhappy
and the skeleton's persuasiveness

in an empty closet. Vista's influence
on a gesture and walk, on sight and speech.
And cry about the unexpected ones
and to the heaven free approach.

Fire in Moscow, war and again
war. Prayers and banners.
A wild mixture of the public and
the Ivanov-Petrov alliance,

mix of the Republics. Dostoevsky.
An ax with the animal on the orbit.
And to the cemetery leads Nevsky
Prospect, and there are wasps instead of warrants.

And net from the childhood
with a gory dead body, and worms in apples,
in plums. An angel by every booth
and by every ravine there is a devil.

And the power is not of the Reds or Gray ones,
and space for the wretched, which is crowded.
And the Sky that is merciless and boundless,
and the cross that is found on the road.

THE VENOUS SNOW, SWOLLEN SNOWDRIFTS

The venous snow, swollen snowdrifts.
Intolerable dark and slush.
You have to close the boundaries of the heart
to have your freedom be bemoaned by speech.

I could have said about sovereignty
to the Trojan horse, to the metal or
to the war, that captured and reigns
the world and there is nothing more.

There is no one any more who wouldn't invade
who wouldn't seize, trample down, cause
pain so hard, that you try to live so badly
you send your language to fight for the cause.

The Webster, Verter, wind were written already.
Already Moscow was burnt and Troy fell.
To meet the Word world is worn out enough already
to open its borders and begin this all.

AUTUMN TIRADE

I haven't been anywhere, besides somewhere,
somehow, don't remember, don't know, whenever.
My memory is bad, since it was harmed
by a wild invasion, by insolent seizure.

My fellow tribesmen became the enemies
and contemporaries too. What can you do?
To make me forget the real name
the tree branch was knocking on the window.

Thus I came over for the time extended,
this is a dark place, remote space,
to hold all of this against myself and
to give up a role of the outcast.

I am guilty for those and for these:
the degree of my guilt is really greater
than a Doctor's degree from Oxford, the guilt is unnoticed
somewhere, somehow by unconscious babble.

I am not entitled to more than God
has given me, because somewhere, somehow
the soul will stand once at the door
step looking at the body of a dead poet.

I am staying. I will not be on the make:
not to grab, take over, not to break
the soul's right to the heavenly name,
the beggar's right to the shepherd's crook.

WINTER TIRADE

All frozen: shrine, barracks, word and reason.
The egg is laid; the cuckoo's fledged and flown,
and now it cuckoos here, there and nowhere.
And can there be a purpose to this rout?

Can there be any sense? Alas there can't.
Winter is folded up beyond the sky.
The world is captive; thought streams through the skin.
Along the whole front not a single tree.

All things join the battle for time, while the
cuckoo keeps a rough tally of the strong;
and as for those who are not, they can lay
no claim to either shelter or defense.

The door slams, the window shakes, the knees are
knocking and the heart cannot endure it.
The eyes stream as though gouged out with a fork;
life crumbles like a poor relation's teeth

So feed the cuckoo's chick with enamel
and into that capacious maw stuff smiles
harvested from an unconscious infant
stripped bare by time.

NO DREAM CAN WAKE YOU UP,
BUT WAKE YOU MUST

No dream can wake you up, but wake you must
and soon.
Life is a warehouse filled with cold
and in the cold there is no room for blame.

Who is that being carried, being buried?
From cold to cold, from darkness into black.
This whole wide world is made of strangers
and an alien time

insists that men must sleep in Baghdad,
that the bromide which the dictator has dispensed
will quiet death for the sake of life,
where hatred is not to blame.

FOR G.G.

From the country of institutes to the country of prostitutes.
The so-and-so is too tired to crack jokes.
Fetters have become a means of living. Ties.
The edge of the world seems narrow to even the narrow-minded.
The edge of light even seems dark to the dark.
So what more is there to wait for other than waiting?
Other than the Coming of God into the grimness?
Other than His Kingdom? Other than the Power and the Glory?

A FRAGMENT OF CULTURE II

                    then the character started being ruined,
hearing got worse, vision fell off.
But what to do if in Sparta
there were no temples or gardens?
But there was the law, otherwise there'd be
the precipice where they threw out the trash.
The pigeons pecked at millet
and the girls strutted wearing beads.
And the girls wanted money,
like birds of peace on a placard.
The person who tied together a common broom
spent an age in someone else's dressing gown.
and the authorities gave out homemade beer
and the guards leered crookedly
in the deserts, where the young men
marched in formation for the prospects of Sparta.
The world was built up anew
and took up almost the whole map.
Life became better, but nature
ran wild and couldn't get used to it.
The blind sullenly walked the map,
the sea answered the deaf.

WINTER LECTURES FOR TERRORISTS

Twenty poems from the novel *Identity Card*

One day in summer, on the shore of Black Sea, I got to know a "terrorist" from the Middle East. Like me, he was relaxing. Or, like me, he was pretending to be on holiday. In fact, neither of us could relax. Nor were either of us liked by everyone. Ten years later I met my terrorist in Jerusalem. He knelt close to me at the Church of St. Peter in Gallicantu. I do not know if he was Catholic or not, but I know that, like me, he was not accepted by the authorities. I know also that he did not attach great importance to it. We are again very similar, remaining human beings — human beings without an appointed place of residence. I was not very surprised when he invited me to give a lecture for people like himself. The next winter I answered that I would try to write something unsuitable. Something unsuitable, in order to kill.

STRATEGY

In order to see
the future,
tear your gaze
from the soil.
Under your feet
are ruins,
splinters of glass,
some sort of bones —
everything that was,
unsuccessfully.
Under your feet
is soil,
on which
you must
firmly stand.

Stand firm
in order
not to die
from fear.

ARRANGING OF SECRET RECESS

Orpheus again
coming down into Hell,
deeper
and deeper
coming down into Hell,
but not finding
even a shadow
of Eurydice.
He does not know
that she was taken
by other terrorists,
and even the shadow
of Eurydice
does not remain after the
explosion of a home-made
bomb,
manufactured
in a suburb
of Moscow.

THEORY OF RECRUITING

Sons of bitches
were born
with hearts of stone,
cherishing this stone
all their life.

Children of
sons of bitches
were born
with hearts of grenade,
in order to
blow to pieces
everything,
and to leave as a message for their descendants —
entrails
(still smoking entrails)
of sons of bitches.

ARMAMENTS OF AN ENEMY

Before in the window
there was a ventilation pane,
to thrust one's head through
and inquire of the passing angels
what was
the hour, day, year, century
from the birth of Christ.
Before, a door
led to the balcony,
and through the room
the cumulus and cirrus
clouds
passed by.
Before, one still
came upon
prophets
on the staircase landings.
Now and then one came upon
prophets.
But now common sense
has won.
Common sense has
definitively won,

whose other side
is too well
known.

SECRET SERVICE

Always something
pricking by abnormality,
wounding by a splinter of deformity —
miserable hearing
or eyesight.
In order to have absolute pitch
it's necessary not to hear.
In order to be sighted
it's necessary not to see
everything
that one can hear
and one can see
on the outside.

Poem *in camera*

Don't take fire in your bare hands,
Don't look down a well without a bottom,
don't knock with a copper ring
on tightly closed souls. Don't do any of this,
and you will not be...
Don't jump at the last minute a train
leaving for destinations unknown,
don't fall from clouds,
don't read between lines,
and you will not be...
Don't search for a wind in a field,
or yesterday on white roads

of the imagination, or beauty in a gutter,
and you will not be...
Don't float against the stream,
Don't recognize belief in mystery
or love of poverty,
and you never will be
the defendant.

CONCEALMENT

Jelly-fish Gorgon
with mirrored dark glasses
made in Poland,
blinded, trudging
relying on the shoulder of
Harvard University's
professor.
Snakes softly hissing
on her head,
which became
myth and globe.
Myth — this is
what exists in salt water
burned by nettle.
In cold sea-water
we have
helpless touches
of former horror —
fully miserable
in front of all
non-mythological.

DISCOVERY OF SHADOWING

1

A man comes crashing,
  comes crashing...
   A man comes crashing
    until he falls
     to his knees.
      What is left
       of the tower
        that appeared
         after him?

2

     The poetry has gone
      from the poetry.
       It spends the night under the tower
        which is just about to fall. Somehow
        there is a connection:
         poetry and the tower,
          the tower and the man,
           from whom poetry has gone.

3

I could say that the tower could not bear heaven's glance.
I could say that the man preferred to see where he was going.
I could say that from poetry nothing has remained, except the tower and the man.
I could say nothing, in view of the fact that the tower, the man, and poetry do not exist.

CLASS-FIGHTS

Small piece of lead —
extremely clear thing.
Clearer
than
human life.

METHODS OF RELATIONS

So the orderlies in dirty overalls
are carrying out
reality
feet first.
So
it returns
from reanimation
in overalls taken
from one of the two
orderlies:
the past or
present.
There is no
orderly future.

RECOMMENDATION OF A GENERAL ORDER

All that is crooked
needs to be straight.
Only that.
Only one proposition —
all make straight
ways for
themselves.

ORIENTATION

From west to east,
from north to south,
from south-west to north-east
and
from east-north to west-south
we are going and going and going
and we see, if we can,
standing
in the waste of heather,
on a cretaceous hill,
in the shadow of Shakespeare,
in a fog of snow and rain
English
to the last degree English
cathedrals of the
XII
XV
XVI
centuries.
They fall from heaven
like bonfires,
trees,
waves,
birds,
but there are no people:
they all refused
to ascend.

DISCOVERY OF IMPORTANT OBJECTS

Looking around
I saw a
nocturnal shadow —
recognized Virgil
holding out

to me
"Hell's guide-book".
I started to read
and discern
districts of one town
and neighborhoods of another.
There were a lot of
familiar names,
so to speak:
vanguard,
carrying on
with his work
in the genre of obituary.
"Our accepted system is
the same as your
accepted system!" —
cried out vanguard
for advertisement.
But in one
artist's cafe
one can find a popular dish —
square eggs,
which symbolize
love.

STUDY OF FOREIGN LANGUAGES

Our faith
is actually atheism:
"God does not exist !"
we say
confidently to
each other.
As if God
Himself
told us about it.
Told us, and
left for the monastery.

JUMPS FROM HEIGHT

A parachute opened
as a butterfly
from Nabokov's collection.
In principle,
a butterfly is the same
as silk —
the jacket
of a Russian bomber.
On the sky nothing
except the ground.
Nothing except the ground.
And a stone
which crumbled to dust
as composed matter
does not draw
attention to anything else.
All of us
will be converted into
dusty butterfly.

MORE RECOMMENDATION OF A GENERAL ORDER

Learn to read
between the lines.
Learn to read
the butterfly
between the lines
of heaven,
in order to understand
what cannot be
understood.

RECONNAISSANCE

During
the war
as before
the swallows fly,
the lilac blooms,
it rains or
it snows,
sometimes
the sun shines,
people are born and die,
in the cafe
they serve
black coffee
in tiny
white
cups,
they pray to God,
feed stray
cats,
dogs,
they read
the Gospel
by Braille,
they lose keys
and find....
At the outbreak of
the six hundred
and sixty-sixth
world
war.

TACTICS

Never look
back.
There, behind,
is war
of a hundred years and a thousand years,
any war.
Don't look back.
There death
pretends to be
Eurydice.
There a man
fights in unconsciousness
for his right
to be called
immortal.

CODE

And now as before
it is necessary
to come and go away,
rinse one's mouth,
clean one's teeth,
wait to be
calculated,
wait to be
released,
and again admitted,
and receive permission
to be in touch with a messenger,
also
to be exposed to danger
to be comprehensible,
put on spectacles

through which it is
impossible to discern the enemy,
and a lot of other things.
And now
I am a guide of shadows,
sensations of
ephemeral.
And now
I am a messenger
between this world
and the next world
which recruited me
from the time
of my birth.
However,
as and wherefore... (further coded) ....

Fugitive Space: Poems 1997-2001

THE CAST-OFF REMNANT OF A CENTAUR

The cast-off remnant of a centaur, on
its pedestal the head sits, turning green,
like Fet's May grass under its little sun,
with fleeting space around and inbetween.
God doesn't wonder, was the creature there,
the way the creature wonders about God.
Where you are now, brazen artificer,
creation needs no legs, and goes unshod.
Where you are now, there is no brass in feet,
no steel in voice, or gesture, or endeavor;
only the purest fluff, to every beat
and every breeze ecstatically aquiver.

FOR P. O.

The snow falls like flakes of plaster
from the firmament, straight out of Giotto.
The heart beats and thuds with a presentiment
as though space is not a thing but a person.

As though it waves a kerchief or something
through the slit and barred windows.
Snow falls longer and shorter
so that indistinctness rules the eyes.

The snow falls but not from the sky—
it lashes and pours, flows and streams.
As though the Coming is being announced
in the wake of pies flavored with glum cinnamon.

WINTER. EUTERPE

1.

A flag in the wind goes mad,
stifling in freedom's air.
It was lately a prison we had:
every day, every year it was there.

When the escort's taken the rest,
Euterpe, what's ours in the end?
Sweet smoke of the ovens, and dust,
blue dust of the fatherland.

2.

The woman who came in winter, the one
they called Euterpe, was always in black.
Kohl shadow on forehead's marble is done
that way, in dressing-rooms off in back.

Before, she'd gone around only in white.
A sea her eyes were, never dry land.
To those who drowned themselves there in delight,
in a language demolishing grammar she sang.

Before, on the threshold she'd always stood,
with arms to the Persian lilacs spread.
The one I once knew is gone for good;
The shade who's come couldn't banish her shade.

3.

Winter. Euterpe. Sleep in a land
one almost doesn't know. As though
I came, outsider to the end,
with barking everywhere I go.

As though I were still on the run,
and had the pack at my heels once more,
As though I felt I couldn't go on
oozing sweat from every pore,

oozing pain. As though I'd not
yet run clear to the very brim
of absence, of non-being, of that
winter that no one could dream.

4.

What's white, Euterpe, can rapidly turn into black.
There's snow in the morning, and then we are wading in mud.
There's God in the morning, and then a conceited pack
of courtiers throws beggars, not changers of money, out.

People at times are indecent in how they behave,
and this is all due to their loving themselves too well.
You're dealing, Euterpe, with a currency that's debased;
the copper you're dealing with no one could now anneal.

I'm sick of philosophy, sick of the smell of decay.
A line from the ashes comes more and more seldom, too,
from the burnt lime, sand, and alien matter that she,
Europa (for she is Euterpe) stirred into the brew.

IT WAS NOT NECESSARY TO STUDY

It was not necessary to study
the language
of a strange country;
anyway, it would be of no help.
It was not necessary to know
where Italy or England
is located;
travel was obviously
out of question.
It was not necessary to live
among the wild beasts
of Noah's ark,
which had just devoured
the last dove of peace,
along with Noah
and his virtuous family.
It was not necessary to strive
for some holy land
awash in milk and honey,
according to rumor.

BUT IF THERE IS A BOMB?

"But if there is a bomb?" —
our question opened
Pandora's box.
"No, there are only
the gifts of the gods,
the beautiful gifts
of the gods," —
answered the Greek woman
with a blinding smile.
Then she went away,
tidying her hair, in order
to bring the next box.

AND NO ONE CAN TELL ABOUT IT

And no one can tell about it,
no one.
What to tell about?
And no one can chant about it,
no one.
What to chant about?
And no one can dance for nobody,
for nobody.
What to dance for?
Everyone, tired of stories,
chants and dances,
retired into his shell,
shut his eyes,
and slept.
Only the head
of John the Baptist,
with wide-open eyes,
looking from the plate
upon the still garrulous,
singing and dancing
daughter of Herodias.

SINCE I HAVE NOT HAD MY HOME

Since I have not had my home
for so long
that my sense of smell is gone,
I spend the nights
in homes of other people.
Lying in strange beds
I dream strangers' dreams,
then escape them
with greatest toil.
My legs, fugitive convicts
bound in boots of time,
do not want to move
across this land any more.
Lacking even paper
I write on my heart
turned inside out.
That is why it squeaks
at night like the earth's axis
that turns me face to face
with the impossible.

OF ALL THINGS TO DO

Of all things to do
there only remained—
to place a sheet of paper
before myself
(of all things to do!).
All others tasks
stepped back
and left me alone
with a white square
pitted and blank.
No other occupations
existed any longer.
In the next world—
where I find myself now—
everyone is writing
white on white,
infinitely writing messages
to favorites,
and tearing them into small
and petty, petty pieces.
And then comes snow.

THAT'S ABOUT IT OR THE THEORY OF RELATIVITY

The corpse of the earth that is
was wrapped in oilcloth
and thrown in midsummer
near a house and forgotten.
The late-autumn rains spill forth,
and the corpse is still there
near a house,
still not identified by the gardener,
who muddles clueless
about what was delivered
with the greatest precaution.
And now it lies thrown
in a heavy wet shroud
of oilcloth near a house,
like any other corpse
of unknown origin
would be thrown in this poor land,
no one desiring to mix it,
in all its fertility,
with any other earth.

DETAIL

Saturday begins on Friday.
I did not manage well
at any of it.
You know now how Lazarus
felt in a coffin.
Transport, certainly, stops.
It is strange that the sun
is not forbidden to ascend.
In streets — empty — clear—
emptiness has settled in,
No Vacancy for life.
Books are without content,
water and grain have no taste,
colors no smell.
In nothing is there meaning.
You think it still Friday evening
but already Saturday has crept in.
No one is around,
as if all have gone into exile.
Transport, certainly, has stopped.
Nothing will wear out,
and nothing is taken out.
Nothing is dug in
and nothing is dug out.
Nothing gathers,
nothing is scattered.
Nothing is born,
nothing dies.
Nothing is remembered,
nothing forgotten.
Nothing begins,
nothing comes to an end.
Nothing doing with the prophet,
nothing without the prophet.
Nothing neither of "no" nor of "not even,"
and never on Saturday,
which is not Sunday.

Ordinary Saturday, empty Saturday,
black Saturday—
whatever you please—
it is before the resurrection.

ANOTHER SIDE OF THE MATTER

Again I have taken a vow of silence,
and immediately broken it,
because the world inside me falls.
I live in smoking ruins
among fragments on which Pushkin
dreamed to read his name
and others' names
(he did not specify which).
Always it happens so
after accidents of consciousness,
as after a flood.
There is nothing more for it:
the angel with the flaming sword
has already expelled me from myself.
Now I cannot come nearer to myself,
and draw the conclusion
that estrangement is equivalent to death.
Tell me, is death too
an experience of life?
You answer with numbers
but I understand only words.
I feel horror before even dates,
every time dying on a different one.
There are no accounts with death,
nor with stars or waves.

IN THE BEGINNING. AT THE END

In the foreseeable future
can anything boundless be expected?
The languages of peoples in diaspora
might as well be crowed by birds.
Such people still dream of a future
favorable to their children.
"The children will be...
they will speak so...
they will not live like we've lived.
The children will be...."
But children do not feel
like children, do not feel
like the future, do not feel
immensity. What do children feel?
Ask them, ask them
what they feel
when daughters of Pharaoh
snare small willow baskets
in vague waters of time.

PRICKED BY THE PIN

Pricked by the pin
you recall words
of St. Thomas Aquinas
to this effect — as many as necessary.
I amend:
as many angels as necessary
to your soul.

THE DIAGNOSIS

1

You yourself will cut off
your ringlets.
Is it for you to be beautiful
when the world is ugly?
You yourself, before a mirror,
you will cut off precisely
lock after lock
in order to see yourself
through God's eyes.

2

You are constantly occupied
with the reconstruction of your brain
so that you do not go mad.
A step forward, a step back—
it's like that at each decision,
at each threshold,
in all of life.
You can't just move!
Sluggishly your schizophrenic life leaks along.
You stop
at every crossing—
the step forward, the step back—
until God pushes you.

I HAVE ROLLED MYSELF UP

I have rolled myself up
into a scroll and sleep.
Only you, Dear,
can unroll me.
Only your heart can read
all that is written
on my palms,
in my eyes.
Only you can know where
to put the full stop.

THE ANATOMICAL POETRY THEATRE

The anatomical poetry theatre
of ancient Uppsala constructs—
would you like to visit it?
It's all laid out there
where there's nothing more
and it is forbidden to be laid out.
All inside out
and they don't sew up wounds of the heart
but make them even deeper,
cut living flesh,
blood gushes like a fountain,
nerves on the surface
and physiology in addition
which is best forgotten
and a whole lot more,
and all this is I, I, I,
a writhing I.
And you say that you yourself
wrote poems when a child
and now, of course,
you could
jostle the old habit into action
in your free time after work.
As though poetry
is measured by time.

IMITATION OF THE ANCIENT

It gets dark late in Palestine, a star
gnaws into the heaven's vault like a woodworm.
The old inhabitants run and cry 'Let's go',
but their unleavened bread remains stale.

No volunteers to bring salt from the sea
and the fruit rots on the wild branch.
I lived in this world: what's it to me?
My hearing is feeble, my eyes not sharp.

I entered where entry was forbidden,
I carried my cross and spat on fashion.
Enemies threatened to break my backbone,
to skin me, bury me, annihilate my kin.

I wore out my seven pairs of steel boots,
wore down seven staffs on alien stones.
I searched the flow of three roads,
knocked on all doors and shutters around.

If someone has forgotten what darkness is
I'll remind them, becoming a heavenly body
in order to light the square and winter upon it
and the Holy Family dressed in white.

COMMEMORATION OF ALEXANDER BLOK

Night melts, exchanging winks
with a star. The brewing of night pales.
Horace's pine-tree walks like the Stone Guest,
down the tear-filled park alleys.

So that a role should appear there
for a poet without pedestals or applause,
less tragic than that of that decadent,
overcoming not just pain but life.

Didn't he give me a sign,
before the baroque threshold, before the abyss
where the rumble of time can only be turned into
poetry by those who are checked over by fate.

FOR I. YEFIMOV

The Flying Dutchman is no longer a flying one, —
It's now laid up. You threw away
the eternity key again
into the refuge of salt.

Let the sea cry with you all along,
the soul's page washed out and
didn't flow into the window
like a winter bird.

What snow writes to her are her thoughts,
what blizzard to her whispers.
And she whispers and writes: I am alone, you are alone,
we're alone in the darkness.

I would like to get frozen, to thaw, to disappear,
before the beginning
of feverish power of metal and fire
and of military green.

Recent Poems 2002-2003

SPRING HARANGUE

For V. L.

Time exists, alas, and like water
torture, drips on your head and tortures
your head, reaching your brain and slowly
reaching your view of the world, where only
you are large, only you, where beside you
there is nothing. Time overrides you,
cuts you down like death and smothers
you, leaving nothing for you or for others.
All that was precious in you and human
time has eroded, devoured, consuming
you in a grave. And tears are worth hardly
the water they're made of. Even a hardy
stoic feels pain when time starts clawing,
like an old fox, at his heart and his lungs.
That is how time has always treated
us, to make us gratefully greet it
up to the grave, to compose odes and sonnets
and to leave signs and marks in its honor.
Its smell is nauseating and ancient,
its stench—a more precise formulation—
soars like a harpy, ready and burning
to seize the nape of the neck, the burdened
head... This is what time is and this is
why I have always struggled against it
down to the bone, using all the measures
that I disposed of, my only treasures—
a star and a bird. And this is also
why I have never trusted all those
who are temporary.

But as for space, space is whiter—
good for gluing trees and the brighter
kinds of flowers to the soil, good for serving
as a map, good for asserting
that on such-and-such a spot and none other
a house shall stand and shield from the weather

the soul, that the soul shall not fear and tremble
at the scarecrows gathered outside the threshold.
The seashore waits for the footstep—the water
waits for the stroke of the arm in order
to splash in reply: "I will come up only
to your knees, so go, go on slowly,
all the way to the edge, to the horizon,
where the stretching sea turns into the rising
sky and its color becomes a little
more vivid." That is the line, the middle,
where I am bound. Beyond that division
there are no graveyards, no morgues, no prisons,
no hospitals, none of that other matter
to which you resign yourself and which shatters
your life into pieces. I hail from the lilac—
a plant on its knees, kneeling and pliant—
a doorway that leads those who enter it onward
toward children and angels, toward signs and wonders,
toward Christ's miracles. Once you enter
it you are part of the Word, its root or
maybe its prefix, it does not really
matter as long as you come to that city
where God is, as long as you reach His climate,
as long as your voice finds a home in His silence.

WHETHER I TURN TO THE SHOOTING STAR OR THE TEAR

Whether I turn to the shooting star or the tear,
whether I wipe the sky or my face...
Farewell to our youth, our bottomless youth —
let its monument be of salt.

A worthless knowledge about the properties of an angle,
about the strength of the rear and the shore.
Our vision has been burned by a needle of ice.
Let the monument be of snow.

Our hearing has been cut, our speech has been sliced,
and the executions have multiplied, in order to nurture
hope and faith in the sword of fire.
Let the monument be of ashes.

WE WILL ALL TURN INTO SALT, AS GOD WISHED

We will all turn into salt, as God wished,
and pay back the oblivion of three roads:
we forgive our youth, maturity and old age
before bodies turn into smoke,

before abandoning the earth's limits,
this black light that is never white,
sewed the edge of the page with black thread
that only a Christ tear could wash away.

IN THE ABSENCE OF CAUSES

If these are wrinkles, then they must be smoothed out,
otherwise time will shrink, turn into the past, and suddenly grow old.
And angles (pieces of light) write down problems for physicists
and particles cover the uncertain phrase, the awkward formula, with earth.

The same tuft on the nape of the neck has a quantum nature (or not?).
The day is dying, the world is becoming more stupid (more smart).
Sawdust is removed from the arenas, the herbarium disappears,
and the hawk turns into a sound.

People without shadows or memories walk around, the clock on the tower
strikes, and its hands whirl in confusion.
Somewhere in the future you (congratulations!) are already in the past,
while the present appears, here and there, through the trees in the forest.

Boundless dreams pull me (captain, what shall I dream?).
I cannot quite remember my number, my black-letter days.
Think of me as an accident, since an accident is guilty
of everything and at all times, guilty without causes.

TO WHOM IT MAY CONCERN:

Consisting as I do of scraps of dreams,
of lands I've never seen, of underpinnings,
of air and salt, of elemental things
unmeddled with by endings or beginnings,

of clay and iron, and of ocean wave
and shingle crowds of feet have trod upon,
of faith and hope, stood at the wall, to brave
the rifles, turning into heavenly stone,

of quiet and simplicity, bestowed
upon us by a woman among women,
of emptiness that stretches like a road
into a vastness where things lose their meaning,

of whisperings, of looking long at that
which goes among us by the name of God,
at death, which never was, and now is not,
at life, of which so little can be had.

EAST NORWALK, CT
From *Northeast States*

The hawk goes corkscrewing into the sky,
drawing with hard quill in three dimensions
on three-ply eternal paper his cry,
his whisper, a faithfulness that's endless.

I see the whole thing, as the neighborhood darkens
and players come in from the playing field—
He cradles the ball like the nape of a girlfriend,
being so strong, and new, and thrilled

with this amorous ruckus, this game, this spat,
this trial and torture of wings, his calling.
The hawk drops down, having built his estate;
a heavy drop of sweat is falling.

Come then, since I have put lips into play,
search out and storm me, unleash a rushing
rain of heavy rough feathers; away,
you stoic of in- and exhalation,

historian of air, soul-striking lightning,
come, take me and lift me far out of sight
of the awful chance that an oath will be broken,
the secret be known of what madness can write.

DIRECTION

To no one beholden, by no one corrupted
The ocean receives the oblivious public
Whose bodies are hurled at the waves, like pebbles,
And repulsed, in undershirts heavy with water.

Once more, and once more, and once more, as in childhood,
When every footstep is under surveillance,
But there's no way back anymore, no returning,
Because to return is to pick up the burden

Of those who decline to swim past the limits
Beyond which each wave carries curled up within it
The white sound of fury, the sound of resistance,
And where you go under to fathom your distance

And discover your time, through salt, not through sunlight,
And come up so your eyes—so your eyes still preserve it,
This darkness, this silence, this bondage, this freedom—
To plunge in the sky like you plunged in the water.

WHAT IS AN APPLE? THE EYE OF THE APPLE

What is an apple? The eye of the apple
Tree. Leaves are the eyelids protecting the eye.
We swore an oath to each other forever,
We gnawed at the granite that grew in the sky.

Tears fell on the ground, and trees without number
Rose on those spots, milk tracing the edge
Of each branch. The eye of the apple tree slumbered.
And daily the green leaves repeated their pledge.

Don't watch how I'm aging. Don't do it. Just love me
On that side of the apple where, back in the days,
I was your orchard, I was your whiteness—
Your whiteness-in-blossom, your oncoming wave.

THE LAST ISLAND

> *Howbeit we must be cast upon a certain island.* Acts 27:26
>
> *There is no lost island merely for the individual.*
> *We are all pieces of the paradise island...* Thomas Merton

1.

That which is prefigured must be figured somewhere. But where?...
And the prodigal son laces his shoes and runs out of the house. He bows his head, he raises his head, he shields his eyes and looks into the distance.
Nothing!
He turns to the road and the wind, to the snow and the rain, to the sun and the moon, to the wave and the stone, to the beast and the bird...
Nothing!
Then he turns to his memory. And his memory leads him back home.
The prodigal son takes off his heavy shoes and crosses the threshold of his old house. He faces his father. He kneels. He looks into his father's eyes and sees in them a new road.

* * *

To tell about miracles. To tell about the laws of the Kingdom of God. To tell about something that no authority, no autocracy, can prohibit. That authority which metes out punishment, which permits no entrance and no exit, which denies human rights and at the same time demands respect.
Once I set out on a journey around my own soul in search of faith, hope, and charity. In search of solid ground. I circled the island of my soul in order to find a world, and I found a person who thought

about God. Then I met another who talked about God. Then another... That is how the island of my soul became filled with people who did not want to leave me, that is how the island of my soul became inhabited. I loved these people, they loved God, and the Lord loved all of us, whether the authorities liked it or not.

* * *

It is difficult to grasp the nature of that which is above your grasp, but it is possible to grasp feelings. Some feelings are lived through poetry, some are lived through prose, and some are lived through both at once.

I first thought of an ISLAND—a place where all those people can come together whose souls have outlines that ideally coincide with the outlines of my own soul—in the Holy Land, which is an island too (even if this goes against common sense and symmetry). These people, who were with me, who took part in my fate, now live inside me in the form of proliferating images and sensations. Hence the hope that we will be together in Eternity as well.

At that time, in the early 1990s, I composed a short essay on the apostolic calling. It was about those who had escaped death and were already celebrating Eternity. But what are those who are still in this world to do, those who want to see what they so fervently desire, the object of their search in a concretely delineated form? It always seems that the ideal does not exist without the real. I, like many others before me, searched for this ideal place both on *gaia*—on the earth—and in the *oikoumene*—in the world known to us. But I could not find it on any map. I found all kinds of other places, even the island of the Artist's Wife, but my island had not been discovered by any crazy sailor, and it had not been mapped by any cartographer.

* * *

Once the possibility of an ideal island had been accepted, the possibility of traveling to this island had to be accepted as well. And as soon as I was allowed to cross borders, I boarded a ferry and set out on a short journey. That is how I found myself in the middle of six-and-a-half thousand Aland Islands, a small number of which turned into poems and were dedicated to the real people of an unreal time. I have no intention to prove that which, according to some, has no proof, and which, according to others, needs no proof. I simply want to say that an island is another reality. It is a place where God is not a fact, but where the only fact is man standing before God.

2.

We are alone in winter's breath and sea. Darkness.
No red-eyed lighthouse winking like a cyclops.
What island is that? What bread and wine is there?
Who is that standing in the field, wandering on trails?

Nothing is known until you have stepped
on this hourglass, like another Odysseus.
How long must we wander, who will support us?
Nothing. Only the wind growing more and more vicious.

Only the wave dragging forward, in our wake,
its black net full of cod and haddock.
And Odysseus looks grim because he needs
an infinity and an eternity to get back to Ithaca.

To get back to anything that is familiar and loved,
to get back to any desire at all
that can be fulfilled only where there is a home
with swallows sketching geometry above the roof.

3.

Only the sea triumphs—the land
retreats if it can.
An island is the face of a clock, where time is deader
because it must turn into water.

You had to be hard and rigid
in order not to spill a single grain
of the quiet sand, where boats were painted
white, blue, and the color of wheat.

You had to become like this in order
to know, departing, that you would not return.
Because the sea is a weakness—where you
beat against waves, as if they were stones.

4.

It blossoms like a flower, if this is how flowers
blossom, if blue or purple roses exist, if they exist
in the middle of winter. In the middle
of lead-and-steel waters, a flame breaks out.

A circle, a ring, and they shout from the ship: "Land, land!"
And they whistle, and sing, and fall silent, and revel, and weep.
The eternal magician has taken off his top hat and said
"voilà!"—and then took out an island, where time has a different
shape.

The world disappears in a crack—and the gangplank is lowered.
It is easier to cross the Rubicon than to live this
life from beginning to end if you are not a scoundrel but a soul
that has fallen asleep in the forest of cradles and ships.

5.

The sea always steps on your heels, on your shadow,
when your back is turned. The loud armies of water
circle the earth in a ring, in order to wash off
the refuse of dirty culture and yesterday's paper.

What shall we see if we squint? The horizon,
the unknown or the primordial. After
discovering man, the island raised an umbrella of pines
above him, never asking for anything in return.

If you swim forward, sooner or later you
will come back. If you swim backward, an island
will appear on your left or your right, an island
gambling with the water for the soul of a sailor or a maiden.

Several thousand years ago, give or take a few days,
boats were sent from the Greeks to the Vikings, to the Vikings
from the Greeks and the Romans, to prove that the way
was round, like an island, and to drink bitter ale from a bucket.

6.

A scrap of paper, a scrap of an island,
with so much already written on it
that the pupil has become permanently
dilated, encompassing the star and the road to the sea.

So that, not just an island, but the whole world
can find a home inside the pupil and on the scrap, a home.
And you have time to say: "Remain with me,
my love, before you turn into foam."

7.

History will end before the other
sciences; every death concludes
a history of roots and
reveals new ground.

In history, war goes on all the time
and numbers are forgotten like dates.
Only geography remains,
like a stain—now white, now blue—a stain.

I have yet to discover a land—
without looking through the shameful lens of the world—
where vision is different and where
there is nothing but life—life, raw and orphaned.

I know that an island has always been waiting for me—
like a final spot and a final circle—
like a star discovered in the mind,
where You unite a friend with a friend.

8.

Again waves follow one another
like questions and answers.
Again the surf, with its white fingers,
erases its traces.

With its long fingers. The
organ is playing again,
round and pebbled with notes,
black and riddled with wounds.

A circular path cannot end.
Another solid ground exists.
You have to blow on the water
to make death recoil.

You have to say: "I
am swimming to God by myself."
The last island. A winter sky.
Salt falls on the grass.

9.

An island, an island's essence. The winds
would be happy to blow on all sides but
they cannot. How could they? They weigh only as much as the pen
I am writing with, only as much

as the waves and the tears. If a swimmer wishes to jump
from the ship into the abyss, to make it to the landing
in time for the beginning he must come back around
to the end. He must tell himself that there is only a handful of solid
ground.

He must head toward a contradictory goal. There,
in the distance, someone pulls him on an invisible rope,
on a ray of light, on a rope held tight in a pierced hand. Here,
he must abandon everything except faith and hope.

10.

My dear son, I write to you from the farthest
point from home.
Even if you have figured out the location of the island,
it is hard to swim alone.

Once we lived in the middle of nowhere, remember?
That is probably why the waves
carried our boat to this island, one of the number
that know Who is the way.

Darkness was left at the edge. Fear and horror
are now off limits.
This island is utterly uninhabited: it has slipped
through the world's fingers.

Do not grieve at our separation:
since we can meet, there will be a meeting.
For the time being, I am stretching
my hands from this island and its infinity.

11.

The sea's oval mirror,
a little murky with age—
where each drop contains a grain of salt
for looking through reality.

In an invisible point in space
light is gathered into a laser bundle—
the stitching, solitary voice
of one who has crossed the current

that runs down the ditch of time. No need any longer
to cry: "I am dying, my Lord!"
And any creature will be glad to offer
you the meat of the grape.

12.

You can discover something in something where you expected
to find nothing. There is an island in the center
of the world. Of the Pontus.
There is a place where fate cannot enter.

Where the curve of space can encompass
anything you like, anything that matters.
Where Ptolemy is friends with Columbus,
both drilling holes in the bottoms of barrels.

There is an island of vowels without consonants,
where in His Power and in His Glory,
God smiled once without remorse—
smiled, and marked the spot with an island.

ABOUT THE AUTHOR

REGINA DERIEVA (1949) has published twenty books of poetry, essays, and prose. Her most recent book is *Sobranie Dorog: selected poems and essays in two volumes*. Her works have been translated into English, Swedish, French, and Italian. A compact disc with her readings in Russian of selected poems was issued in 1999. Derieva's work has appeared in the *Modern Poetry in Translation, Poetry East, Cross Currents, Ars-Interpres, Salt, Notre Dame Review* as well as in many Russian magazines. She has translated poetry by Thomas Merton and contemporary American, Australian and British poets. Regina currently lives in Sweden.

ABOUT THE TRANSLATORS

ILYA BERNSTEIN lives in New York City. He is the author of one book of poems, *Attention and Man* (Ugly Duckling Presse, 2003). His translations of Daniil Kharms have appeared in *Ars-Interpres*, and his writings on art history have been published in the magazine *RES*. He is currently working on a one-act play, *An Hour and Fifteen Minutes*.

Kevin Carey is a poet and translator. He was born in 1952 in Ohio. He was educated at Williams College, MA, and at Georgetown University, Washington, D.C. For some years he has been a member of the US diplomatic corps. His work and translations have appeared in *Cross Currents* and *Modern Poetry in Translation*.

PETER FRANCE, who recently retired from a chair in French at Edinburgh University, has translated collections of poems by Gennady Aygi, Joseph Brodsky, Vladimir Mayakovsky and (with Jon Stallworthy) Alexander Blok and Boris Pasternak. He is author of *Poets of Modern Russia* (1982) and the editor of the *Oxford Guide to Literature in English Translation* (2000).

ANDREY GRITSMAN is a native of Moscow. He emigrated from the Soviet Union in 1981 and currently lives in the New York City area. He is a poet, translator and essayist, and the author of six books of poetry, including *Long Fall* from Spuyten Duyvil. His work has appeared in the *Manhattan Review, Poetry International, Synaestetic, Poetry New York* and *Modern Poetry in Translation*. Andrey runs a popular Intercultural Poetry Series at the fabulous Cornelia Street Café in New York City.

RICHARD MCKANE started writing poetry and translating it in 1967, while studying Russian at Oxford University. His first book (Penguins and OUP 1969) was *Selected Poems of Anna Akhmatova*. A vastly expanded edition was published by Bloodaxe Books in 1989. He has also published (co-translated with Elizabeth McKane) *The Moscow Notebooks and Voronezh Notebooks* (Bloodaxe, reissuing 2003) and *The Pillar of Fire, Selected Poems of Nikolay Gumilyov* (Commentary by Michael Basker with Anvil Press 1999). He edited and was main translator of the anthology *Ten Russian Poets: Surviving the Twentieth Century* (Anvil Press 2003).

ROBERT REID is a Reader in Modern Languages (Russian) at Keele University. He has written and edited many books and articles on Romanticism and is co-editor of *Essays in Poetics*, the journal of the British Neo-formalist Circle, to which he has also regularly contributed translations of modern Russian poetry. He has translated Russian poetry for various collections and anthologies.

ALAN SHAW is a dramatist and composer as well as a poet, translator, and critic. He has published translations of Pushkin's *Mozart and Salieri* and Griboyedov's *The Woes of Wit*. His poems have appeared in *Grand Street* and *Partisan Review*, and his essays in *Hudson Review, Michigan Quarterly Review*, and *ebr* (electronic book review). In both his poetic practice and in his criticism he has been interested in the use of verse as a dramatic and narrative medium, as well as in musical text-setting and the relation of verse to music.

SPUYTEN DUYVIL

ISBN	Title	Author
1881471772	6/2/95	DONALD BRECKENRIDGE
193313223X	8TH AVENUE	STEFAN BRECHT
1881471942	ACTS OF LEVITATION	LAYNIE BROWNE
1933132221	ALIEN MATTER	REGINA DERIEVA
1881471748	ANARCHY	MARK SCROGGINS
1881471675	ANGELUS BELL	EDWARD FOSTER
188147142X	ANSWERABLE TO NONE	EDWARD FOSTER
1881471950	APO/CALYPSO	GORDON OSING
1933132248	APPLES OF THE EARTH	DINA ELENBOGEN
1881471799	ARC: CLEAVAGE OF GHOSTS	NOAM MOR
1881471667	ARE NOT OUR LOWING HEIFERS SLEEKER THAN NIGHT-SWOLLEN MUSHROOMS?	NADA GORDON
0972066276	BALKAN ROULETTE	DRAZAN GUNJACA
1881471241	BANKS OF HUNGER AND HARDSHIP	J. HUNTER PATTERSON
1881471624	BLACK LACE	BARBARA HENNING
1881471918	BREATHING FREE	VYT BAKAITIS (ED.)
1881471225	BY THE TIME YOU FINISH THIS BOOK YOU MIGHT BE DEAD	AARON ZIMMERMAN
1881471829	COLUMNS: TRACK 2	NORMAN FINKELSTEIN
0972066284	CONVICTION & SUBSEQUENT LIFE OF SAVIOR NECK	CHRISTIAN TEBORDO
1881471934	CONVICTIONS NET OF BRANCHES	MICHAEL HELLER
1881471195	CORYBANTES	TOD THILLEMAN
1881471306	CUNNING	LAURA MORIARTY
1881471217	DANCING WITH A TIGER	ROBERT FRIEND
1881471284	DAY BOOK OF A VIRTUAL POET	ROBERT CREELEY
1881471330	DESIRE NOTEBOOKS	JOHN HIGH
1881471683	DETECTIVE SENTENCES	BARBARA HENNING
1881471357	DIFFIDENCE	JEAN HARRIS
1881471802	DONT KILL ANYONE, I LOVE YOU	GOJMIR POLAJNAR
1881471985	EVIL QUEEN	BENJAMIN PEREZ
1881471837	FAIRY FLAG AND OTHER STORIES	JIM SAVIO
1881471969	FARCE	CARMEN FIRAN
188147187X	FLAME CHARTS	PAUL OPPENHEIMER
1881471268	FLICKER AT THE EDGE OF THINGS	LEONARD SCHWARTZ
1933132027	FORM	MARTIN NAKELL
1881471756	GENTLEMEN IN TURBANS, LADIES CAULS	JOHN GALLAHER
1933132132	GESTURE THROUGH TIME	ELIZABETH BLOCK
1933132078	GOD'S WHISPER	DENNIS BARONE
1933132000	GOWANUS CANAL, HANS KNUDSEN	TOD THILLEMAN
1881471586	IDENTITY	BASIL KING
1881471810	IN IT WHATS IN IT	DAVID BARATIER
0972066233	INCRETION	BRIAN STRANG
0972066217	JACKPOT	TSIPI KELLER
1881471721	JAZZER & THE LOITERING LADY	GORDON OSING
1881471926	KNOWLEDGE	MICHAEL HELLER
193313206X	LAST SUPPER OF THE SENSES	DEAN KOSTOS
1881471470	LITTLE TALES OF FAMILY AND WAR	MARTHA KING
0972066241	LONG FALL	ANDREY GRITSMAN
0972066225	LYRICAL INTERFERENCE	NORMAN FINKELSTEIN
1933132094	MALCOLM AND JACK	TED PELTON
1933132086	MERMAID'S PURSE	LAYNIE BROWNE
1881471594	MIOTTE	RUHRBERG & YAU (EDS.)
097206625X	MOBILITY LOUNGE	DAVID LINCOLN
1881471322	MOUTH OF SHADOWS	CHARLES BORKHUIS
1881471896	MOVING STILL	LEONARD BRINK
1881471209	MS	MICHAEL MAGEE
1881471853	NOTES OF A NUDE MODEL	HARRIET SOHMERS ZWERLING
1881471527	OPEN VAULT	STEPHEN SARTARELLI
1933132116	OSIRIS WITH A TROMBONE ACROSS THE SEAM OF INSUBSTANCE	JULIAN SEMILIAN
1881471977	OUR DOGS	SUSAN RING
1881471152	OUR FATHER	MICHAEL STEPHENS

0972066209	OVER THE LIFELINE	ADRIAN SANGEORZAN
1933132256	PIGS DRINK FROM INFINITY	MARK SPITZER
1881471691	POET	BASIL KING
0972066292	POLITICAL ECOSYSTEMS	J.P. HARPIGNIES
1933132051	POWERS: TRACK 3	NORMAN FINKELSTEIN
1933132191	RE-TELLING	TSIPI KELLER
1881471454	RUNAWAY WOODS	STEPHEN SARTARELLI
1933132035	SAIGON & OTHER POEMS	JACK WALTERS
1933132167	SARDINE ON VACATION	ROBERT CASTLE
1881471888	SEE WHAT YOU THINK	DAVID ROSENBERG
1933132124	SHEETSTONE	SUSAN BLANSHARD
1881471640	SPIN CYCLE	CHRIS STROFFOLINO
1881471578	SPIRITLAND	NAVA RENEK
1881471705	SPY IN AMNESIA	JULIAN SEMILIAN
1933132213	STRANGE EVOLUTIONARY FLOWERS	LIZBETH RYMLAND
188147156X	SUDDENLY TODAY WE CAN DREAM	RUTHA ROSEN
1933132175	SUNRISE IN ARMAGEDDON	WILL ALEXANDER
1881471780	TEDS FAVORITE SKIRT	LEWIS WARSH
1933132043	THINGS THAT NEVER HAPPENED	GORDON OSING
1933132205	THIS GUY	JAMES LEWELLING
1933132019	THREE MOUTHS	TOD THILLEMAN
1881471365	TRACK	NORMAN FINKELSTEIN
188147190X	TRANSGENDER ORGAN GRINDER	JULIAN SEMILIAN
1881471861	TRANSITORY	JANE AUGUSTINE
1933132140	VIENNA ØØ	EUGENE K. GARBER
1881471543	WARP SPASM	BASIL KING
188147173X	WATCHFULNESS	PETER O'LEARY
1881471993	XL POEMS	JULIUS KELERAS
0972066268	YOU, ME, AND THE INSECTS	BARBARA HENNING

All Spuyten Duyvil titles are available
through your local bookseller via *Booksense.com*

Distributed to the trade by
Biblio Distribution
a division of NBN
1-800-462-6420
http://bibliodistribution.com

All Spuyten Duyvil authors may be contacted at
authors@spuytenduyvil.net

Author appearance information and background at
http://spuytenduyvil.net